Unit 7
The Reformation
Shifts in Power
Reader

GRADE 5

Core Knowledge Language Arts®

Core Knowledge®

Contents

The Reformation
Shifts in Power
Reader

Chapter 1

The Power of the Printed Word

THE BIG QUESTION
Why was Gutenberg's invention of a printing press so important?

Did you know that a man named "John Gooseflesh" changed the world? Johann Gensfleisch, which in English is John Gooseflesh, was born in the city of Mainz, Germany, around 1397 CE. However, by the time Johann started school, he went by the name *Gutenberg* instead of *Gensfleisch* and that is the name we remember. Gutenberg was the name of the large manor house in which Johann grew up. He came from a very wealthy family.

Johann was taught to read from an early age. Unlike the homes of less privileged children in the early 1400s, the Gutenberg house was full of books. That may not seem unusual, but it was. Books in the 1400s were very different from the books we have today. The book you are reading right now is a printed book. There are thousands of copies of this book, all exactly the same. They were printed by machines in a very short time. Not so with the books in Johann's day. Each book in the Gutenberg's home library was one of a kind, rare, and expensive.

Books in the Middle Ages

Throughout the Middle Ages, books were made by hand. Much of the writing was done by monks working in monasteries, although the craft of making books also took place in some universities and **secular** schools. Primarily existing books such as the Bible and great works authored by ancient Greek and Roman scholars were copied. The monks painstakingly copied the text with pen and ink on thin sheets of **parchment**.

Flemish illuminated manuscript, 1365 CE

It typically took monks many weeks or months to complete the pages of an entire book. The highest quality books were illustrated. This task was accomplished by a skilled artist called an illuminator. An illuminator decorated the pages with colorful, ornate designs and small pictures. Bits of gold, pounded very thin, were applied to the pages of the most expensive books to make the text and illustrations shine.

When the manuscript was finished, the final step was to **bind** the pages into a book. This was done by sewing them together along one side and then sandwiching them between wooden boards covered with cloth or leather.

An enormous amount of time and effort went into creating each book. Only the wealthiest members of society, scholars, and Church **clergy** could afford to own such treasures. Throughout the Middle Ages, of course, these were typically the only people who were able to read.

Lead and Letters

When Johann Gutenberg finished school, he went to work at the mint in Mainz. His father was in charge of the mint, which coined money for the city. Johann learned how to melt and cast metal in molds to form precise shapes. He liked working with metal, and he was skilled at metal casting.

As Johann Gutenberg grew older and became a master metalsmith, he thought a lot about the growing demand for books. His experience working with metal gave him an idea: what if he cast letters out of a metal such as lead? He could arrange those metal letters, or pieces of type, in lines to spell out words, make sentences, and create entire pages of text. By applying ink to the surface of the type and pressing paper onto it, he could print those pages.

Gutenberg set out to try. First, he developed a way to pour melted lead into molds in the shapes of the letters of the alphabet. Each letter (piece of type) was cast as a mirror image of how it would look when printed. For example, "R" was cast as "Я," and "C" was cast as "Ɔ ." Gutenberg made many copies of each letter, both capital and lowercase, plus every punctuation mark. Because his collection of metal type was made up of individual pieces that could be moved around to form endless combinations of letters, it was called movable type.

Movable type

Gutenberg's printing press, 1430 CE

Gutenberg didn't truly invent movable type. The Chinese and Koreans had used a form of movable type hundreds of years earlier. He didn't invent printing, either. Different printing techniques had also existed for centuries. In Europe, people had begun printing with ink on paper using blocks of wood. This technique called woodblock or woodcut printing began around 1400 CE. The surface of a block of wood was carved to create raised letters and images. Ink was then applied to the carved surface. Finally, the block was pressed onto paper to make a print. If you've ever pressed your thumb onto an inkpad and then touched it to paper, you've created a "thumbprint" in much the same way. Woodblock printing was a complex and time-consuming process. It wasn't much faster than copying pages of text by hand!

What Johann Gutenberg did invent was a machine that greatly improved the process of printing with movable type. He may have gotten the idea for his press from a winepress, a machine used to press the juice

Movable type from China

A woodcut print, 1480 CE

out of grapes. Gutenberg's printing press worked in a similar way. Instead of squeezing grapes, though, his press squeezed paper against the inked surface of metal type to make a clear, dark imprint of words on paper. Once he had perfected both his metal type and his press, he was able to print—with help from a number of assistants—several hundred pages a day.

Gutenberg's Bible

After experimenting with printing a few official documents and small, simple books of grammar, Gutenberg was ready to undertake a big project. He decided to print a large, beautiful Bible. He hoped to make a lot of money. Gutenberg started printing his Bible around 1450 CE. He may have cast more than 100,000 pieces of type for it. Several times during the process he ran out of money and had to borrow more. He completed the first edition of roughly 180 copies of the Bible (the exact number isn't really known) in 1454 or 1455 CE. Gutenberg's Bible was the first large book printed with movable metal type in Europe.

The Power of Communication

Gutenberg didn't make much money from his Bible or his new printing process. But as you read at the beginning of this chapter, he did change the world. Gutenberg's printing press and the availability of inexpensive paper made it possible to produce many copies of books and documents quickly. This dramatically lowered the price of books and other printed materials. Suddenly, people had a way to distribute ideas and information from person to person, and place to place, much faster than ever before.

Soon printing presses just like Gutenberg's were producing hundreds and then thousands of books in cities throughout Europe. At first, most books were printed in Latin. But it wasn't long before books were being printed in more familiar languages including French, English, Italian, Spanish, and German.

At this time too, literacy, or the ability to read and write, increased across Europe. A growing middle class of merchants and craftsmen gained both wealth and influence. Learning to read and write became something more and more people wanted, and needed, to do. As a result, the demand for books increased. Books and other printed materials were more readily available for those people who could read.

Today, you can walk into a library or bookstore and choose from thousands of books. You can download books from the Internet to laptops, tablets, and phones. So you have to use your imagination to really appreciate

Page from Gutenberg's Bible, printed between 1454 and 1456 CE

Incipit liber bresich quē nos genesi

In principio creauit deus celū dicit
et terram. Terra autem erat inanis
vacua: et tenebre erāt sup faciē abissi
et sps dni ferebat sup aquas. Dixit
deus. Fiat lux. Et facta e lux. Et vid
deus lucem qp esset bona: ⁊ diuisit lu
a tenebris. appellauitq; lucem diem
tenebras noctem. Factūq; est vespe
mane dies vnus. Dixit qz deus. Fi
firmamentū in medio aquaz: ⁊ dii
dat aquas ab aquis. Et fecit deus fi
mamentū: diuisitq; aquas que erā
sub firmamento ab hijs q̄ erant sup
firmamentū. et factū e ita. Vocauitq
deus firmamentū celū: ⁊ factū e vesp
et mane dies secūd9. Dixit vero deus
Congregent aque que sub celo sūt i
locū vnū ⁊ appareat arida. Et factū
ita. Et vocauit deus aridam terram

just how big a change Gutenberg and his printing press brought about. Before Gutenberg, very few people had ever held, let alone read, a book. After Gutenberg, books were much more common. Gutenberg's printing press **revolutionized** communication, much like the Internet revolutionized how people communicated in the second half of the 1900s—although at not quite the same lightning speed! Plentiful, affordable books opened the door to a whole new world of learning and ideas.

Some people didn't like this turn of events, however. Some government officials worried: what if printing presses are used to spread ideas that weaken our power over the people? Some leaders of the Catholic Church thought: what if the presses are used to publish ideas that contradict Church **doctrine**?

But no one could stop the presses and the sudden flow of information and ideas. It is true to say that Gutenberg revolutionized communication. And just as some political and religious leaders feared, big changes certainly did lie ahead.

Upper and Lowercase

Have you ever heard someone call capital letters "uppercase" letters or small letters "lowercase" letters? These terms got their start in early printing shops like Gutenberg's. A person called a typesetter arranged the individual pieces of type into the whole block of type that would be printed to create a page of text. This person grabbed pieces of type from two boxes, or cases, usually stacked one on top of the other. The upper case held the capital letters, while the lower case held the small letters. The names *uppercase* and *lowercase* caught on, and have survived for more than 500 years!

Type stored in cases

Parchment vs. Paper

The ancient Egyptians produced paper from the stems of the papyrus plant. Much later, the Chinese developed another way of producing paper. The Chinese method involved placing plant fibers in water to produce a pulp that could be pressed and dried into thin sheets. The art of papermaking slowly made its way across Asia into Europe. By the 1200s, there were paper mills in Spain and Italy.

In medieval Europe, paper was made primarily from linen rags. The rags were repeatedly soaked in water and beaten to create a pulp of tiny linen fibers. Papermakers dipped frames made of wire mesh into the pulp to capture a thin layer of these fibers, forming a sheet of paper. The sheets were dried and pressed, and sometimes polished with a smooth stone to create a soft, shiny surface. Compared to parchment, paper was lightweight and relatively inexpensive. Paper was often used for making small volumes of sermons and low-cost textbooks, whereas high-quality books were almost always produced using parchment. However, after the invention of the printing press, paper largely replaced parchment.

German papermakers in the 1600s

Chapter 2

Letters Come Alive!

THE BIG QUESTION
How did the printing press affect the lives of ordinary people?

"Hurry up, Jacques. We can't afford to keep Monsieur Lafarge waiting," came the sound of a stern voice.

Jacques tried to match his father's long strides as they walked through the narrow back streets of Paris. From time to time they came upon merchants who stood in their doorways, hawking their wares: cloth, pots and pans, leather goods, and books. As they passed a stack of books on a bookseller's table, Jacques couldn't help but stop. He ran his fingertips across the covers with their mysterious markings.

"What do you fancy, young man?" asked the shopkeeper, stepping up. "A book of prayers, or stories of brave knights and their incredible adventures?"

Jacques shook his head and backed away. Even if he had a few coins, there was no point in buying books. The markings—the letters—made no sense to him. He had begged his parents to send him to school so he could learn to read and write, but there was never enough money.

"Jacques!" His father's voiced boomed out above the noise of the street.

Jacques sprinted to catch up. "Sorry, Father, I was just—" said Jacques, panting as he spoke.

"You must make a good impression. A chance like this won't come again," his father explained.

Jacques nodded as they turned a corner. He knew what an opportunity this was. His father's cousin, Lafarge, owned a printing shop, one of the

newest in the city. Lafarge had agreed to take Jacques on. Jacques would be cleaning, running errands, and doing whatever he was told, but he would also get to see a printing press in action and learn how books were made. This job might even lead to an apprenticeship. The thought filled Jacques with excitement. But it terrified him, too. What if reading was essential to working at the shop? What would happen if Lafarge found out that he couldn't read?

Jacques tried to put that thought out of his mind as his father stopped abruptly in front of a large wooden door. Jacques's fingers tightened around the bag that contained the few possessions he owned. Gripping it with white-knuckled hands, he followed his father into the shop.

Light from a number of windows lit the spacious interior. A sharp smell, like paint or varnish, filled the air. A dark-haired boy carried a huge stack of paper in his arms. He looked a few years older than Jacques, perhaps sixteen. A large desk with a slanted top stood on one side of the room. A stooped, gray-haired man stood in front of it. He was picking out small squares of metal from cases above the desk and assembling them in a long, wooden tray. His fingers moved very quickly.

Impressive as that was, it was the wooden **contraption** in the middle of the room that took Jacques's breath away. This must be the press, he thought, the new invention everyone was talking about.

He'd heard rumors that it could print whole pages at a time—and make many copies in minutes. Jacques thought the press looked a little like the winepresses he had seen in the countryside. It had a large, screw-like **mechanism** in the center and a wooden **lever** as thick as Jacques's arm. Two men—one tall, one short—were huddled around the press, studying something Jacques could not see. The tall man looked up and caught sight of them. He grinned broadly at Jacques's father.

"Cousin!" he shouted, coming toward them. He shook hands with Jacques's father and looked down at Jacques with piercing eyes. "You would be Jacques, of course," the tall man continued. "I hope you will prove to be as good a worker as your father promised me you would be."

"I will work extremely hard, Monsieur," Jacques said, "at whatever task you give me."

"Excellent! Now meet your fellow workers," Lafarge replied. His muscular arm swept toward the gray-haired man. "My typesetter, Henri. The best in the business," he exclaimed loudly. Turning toward the press, Lafarge gestured toward a young man and the dark-haired boy. "Philippe, my head printer, and his apprentice, Jean-Claude," Lafarge exclaimed. Then he gave a short nod, as if enough time had been wasted. "Jean-Claude will show you what to do," Lafarge concluded before marching away.

Jacques hardly had time to say goodbye to his father before Jean-Claude was leading him toward a back room. He pointed toward a corner where a broom stood beside a pail and a pile of clean rags.

"Monsieur insists on a spotless shop. The rags are for cleaning type," explained Jean-Claude.

Jacques wasn't sure what type was or how it was to be cleaned, but he just nodded. He didn't want to look foolish.

Broom in hand, Jacques started sweeping in a far corner of the shop. As he worked, Jacques observed what was happening around him. He hoped to learn as much as he could. Each time customers came in, Lafarge rushed over to greet them. He guided them into a small office where a discussion ensued. Jacques caught snatches of conversations about books, pamphlets, law certificates, and decrees. People wanted all sorts of things printed.

Jacques swept his way over to where Henri was working and watched the old man out of the corner of his eye. He had filled a large wooden frame with rows and rows of the little pieces of metal. Jacques realized they must be letters, what Jean-Claude had called type. Henri's job seemed to be to arrange the letters—the type—to form words. Obviously Henri knew how to read. The thought made Jacques uneasy.

Henri suddenly lifted up the frame full of type and spun around, nearly knocking into Jacques. "Out of the way, boy," the typesetter yelled.

Jacques flattened himself against the nearest wall. But he watched as Philippe helped Henri set the tray of metal pieces into the press and clamp it into place. Behind them, Jean-Claude smeared what looked like shiny black paste onto a board. "Ink!" thought Jacques. Jean-Claude then grabbed two rounded balls of leather topped with handles. He pressed the balls against the plate of ink, and then dabbed their blackened bottoms on the type held tightly in the frame. Jacques could see the surface of the type turn dark as the layer of ink grew thicker.

Philippe stepped in, holding a large sheet of cream-colored paper by its edges. Working together, the three men gently fitted the paper into the press so it lay on top of the type. Then Philippe grabbed the huge lever that jutted out from the side of the press. He pulled it toward him with a powerful, even stroke. The great screw in the center of the press turned. A flat, wooden board **descended**, pressing the paper down onto the inked type beneath it.

Jacques forgot all about staying out of the way. He sensed something remarkable was about to happen. He stepped closer to the press as Philippe released the lever. Jean-Claude reached in and lifted up the paper. Perfect rows of black letters stood out against its creamy surface. Jacques thought it was the most beautiful thing he had ever seen.

"That's amazing!" he blurted out. "It's like magic."

Both Philippe and Jean-Claude grinned at him. But Henri scowled and shook his finger. "Get to work, boy. If Monsieur Lafarge sees you dawdling, you'll be out of a job," he barked.

Jacques flushed with embarrassment and went back to sweeping. Jean-Claude and Philippe seemed nice enough. But Henri obviously didn't care for him. He would need to stay out of the old man's way.

Jacques grew used to the flow of the work and the captivating **rhythm** of the press. One printed sheet after another came to life inside it. Each sheet of paper was hung up to dry, clipped to cords that ran across the back of the shop like laundry lines. Once, when he was sure Henri was not looking, Jacques stepped up and stared closely at one. The letters were perfectly aligned and elegantly shaped. But he had no idea what was written on that beautiful page because he didn't know which letters were which or how they could be combined into words. He stared and stared at the mysterious shapes, feeling more hopeless than ever.

When Jacques finished sweeping, he helped Jean-Claude bring in a load of paper that had just arrived. After lunch, Philippe asked him to stir a new batch of ink. The stuff was as dark and sticky as tar, but Jacques liked the smell of it. "It's made of lampblack, varnish, and egg white," Philippe explained. "There's also powdered metals that help the ink to cling to the type and not spread into the fibers of the paper."

Jacques stirred the ink until the muscles in his arms ached. But he forgot the pain when Philippe praised his good work. By late afternoon Jacques was feeling good about his first day. Then suddenly Henri called to him from across the room. "Boy, come here!" he yelled. Nervously, Jacques went over and stood beside the typesetter's slanted desk.

"This type needs cleaning," Henri said, handing Jacques a basket of metal pieces thick with ink. "Wipe them until they shine."

In the back room, Jacques polished the pieces of type until they gleamed. He returned to Henri and held out the basket.

"All done, sir," announced Jacques proudly.

But Henri didn't take the basket. Instead he gestured toward the many small compartments in the cases above his desk. "Put the letters back where they belong," he ordered.

Jacques's heart sank. He glanced up at the cases and then down at the basket of type in his hands. He had no idea which letters were which. He set the basket on the desk, plucked out a piece of type, and pretended to study it while **shame** turned his cheeks crimson. He knew the typesetter was watching him even more closely. Finally, Jacques summoned up the courage to look the old man in the eyes. "I'm sorry. I can't do it, sir," he said in a voice that was almost a whisper.

Henri took the piece of type from Jacques. "I knew that already. This was a test," Henri replied.

"You knew? How? I tried so hard!" said Jacques, all the while struggling to stop his voice from trembling.

The old man's reply was quiet and kind. "Yes, you did. But when you gazed up at the drying sheets of paper, you simply stared at them. If you'd been reading the words printed on them, your eyes would have moved from side to side," he explained.

"I see," Jacques sighed, feeling his shoulders sag. "And now I have failed your test as well."

"Oh, no, Jacques, you passed my test quite nicely," said the old man with a smile.

Jacques looked up sharply. "But I . . . ," he stuttered.

"You were truthful," Henri said, interrupting. "That is as important as being able to read. At least as far as I am concerned."

"But I can't see how I can learn to read, sir," exclaimed Jacques. "I have no money for school."

"Then it's a good thing you have me," Henri replied. The old man picked a piece of type from the case. He dabbed a bit of ink onto its surface and pressed it gently against the back of Jacques's hand.

"That is the letter 'J.' It is the first letter of your name. Tomorrow you will begin learning all the others," he said calmly.

Jacques touched the ink mark on his hand. "Why?" he asked. "Why would you do this for me?"

"Because I remember how it felt not to be able to read," the old man replied. Then Henri put a hand on Jacques's shoulder. "This morning, when you saw your first sheet come off the press, you said it was magic. It is, in a way. But the greater magic is reading. The ability to read will change the world. You mark my words, Jacques!"

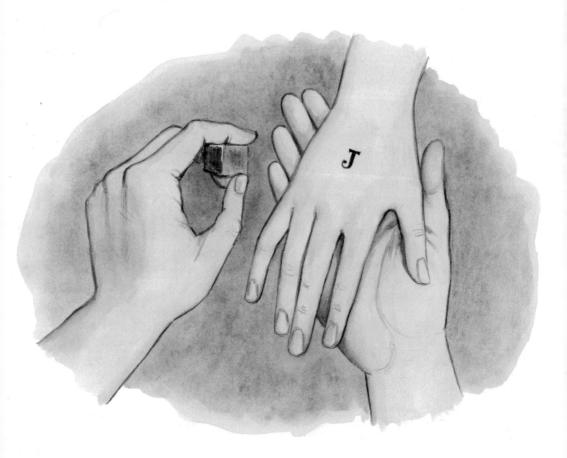

Chapter 3

Setting the Stage for Reform

THE BIG QUESTION

Why did some people believe the Church needed to be reformed during the 1400s and 1500s?

Gutenberg's printing press did change the world: at least the European world. But before we talk about the changes that took place in Europe in the 1500s, let's journey further back in time.

You may remember that after the fall of Rome in 476 CE, there was no longer a strong government to unite people in different countries. Instead, the Catholic Church took control. It soon became the largest and most powerful **institution** in western Europe. The Church united people through a common belief in the Christian God and the Christian promise of heaven.

The Church was very important to Europeans in the Middle Ages. It was the social glue that held communities together. It provided instruction on how to live in this world and how to get to the next world. The Church gave comfort and protection to those in need. The Church was also largely responsible for educating those fortunate enough to receive an education.

If you had lived during this period in history, the Catholic Church would have been a major focus in your life. Typically once a week, you would have gone to church to attend Mass. Mass is the central act of worship in the life of a Catholic. Depending on where you lived, the church you attended might have been an especially large and beautiful cathedral. Cathedrals were among the most impressive buildings in medieval Europe and would have been a constant reminder of the Church's presence, power, and wealth. Most people, however, attended a much smaller local church.

Notre Dame Cathedral,
Paris, France

Latin and Learning

Latin was the language of the Church. The priest conducted Mass entirely in Latin. Songs sung in church—by choirs, not the **congregation**—had Latin words. The Bible, too, was written in Latin. The problem was, only the Church's clergy and the most educated people in society could speak, read, and understand Latin. For everyone else, Latin was a foreign language. Imagine going to church your entire life and never knowing exactly what was being said or sung!

Since most people could not read or write, the local church was their main source of instruction with regard to Church teachings. One of the most important teachings was that the Church provided the only path to heaven. People who disobeyed or opposed Church teachings risked punishment. If they persisted in doing something wrong, or in holding to beliefs that did not follow Church doctrine, and refused to **recant**, they could be accused of **heresy**. A person charged with heresy could be excommunicated. This meant that a person's membership in the Christian community was cut off—and so, people believed, was their access to heaven. In some cases, heresy was punishable by death.

...at terra nra : tante uirginis
ta conceptu. Hec est enim flo-
: de qua ortum est preciosum lil
nuallium. Per cuis partu mutat
ta : plasforum qz dicatur   culp
um est in ea illud eue in feliciat
um. in tristicia paries filios : qui
lecicia dnm parturiu. Eua eni
exultauit. Eua lacrimas. mar
nte gaudiu portauit : quia illa
coicit inocentem. Uirgo quip

Growing Power and Influence

Throughout the Middle Ages, the power of the Church continued to grow. Part of the reason behind this increasing power was money. Christians were not simply supposed to obey the Church, but they were also expected to support it financially. Everyone was expected to give a portion of their yearly earnings to the Church. The money (or goods, such as crops and livestock) was paid like a tax and called a tithe.

Over time, the Church became very rich. It owned land, buildings, and even parts of towns. Wealthy people **bequeathed** land and money to the Church. This wealth gave the pope, who was the leader of the Church, political as well as religious power.

Questionable Practices

For some time, the Church had raised money by issuing certificates that could release or pardon people from penance. Penance was the punishment that the Church taught was due after a **sin** was **confessed** and forgiven. Previously, penance had to be performed *before* a sin was forgiven. These certificates were called indulgences. Technically, indulgences weren't sold; they were given in exchange for donations of money. Nevertheless, the money raised by the issuing of indulgences became a huge business for the Church. Many other corrupt practices also increased, such as the ability of wealthy people to buy their way into the clergy. In the late 1400s and early 1500s, religious reformers spoke out against corrupt practices in the Church and demanded reform.

An indulgence certificate from John, abbot of Abingdon, to Henry Lanley and his wife Katherine, 1476 CE

The Beginning

The word *reform* means to make changes to something in order to improve it. In European history, the Reformation, or the Protestant Reformation as it is also called, was a reform movement that challenged the Catholic Church. The movement challenged the Church's teachings and authority and demanded the reform of certain practices. The Reformation began as a religious debate but quickly grew into something much larger. It laid the foundation for what would eventually become known as Protestantism—one of the three major branches of Christianity. The other branch of Christianity, the Orthodox Church, was formed hundreds of years earlier. Now the Reformation would bring about Protestantism. In addition, the Reformation led to great political and social change throughout much of Europe.

One reformer in particular helped usher in the Reformation. His name was Martin Luther. Luther was a German monk and a **devout** Catholic. Yet the corruption he saw in the Church, along with his personal ideas about **salvation**, turned him against it. Luther's dispute with the Church succeeded, at least in part, because of the printing press.

Martin Luther painted by Lucas Cranach the Elder, 1532 CE

Shifts in Power

As a result of the Reformation, Europe experienced unrest, **persecution**, and several wars. However, Europe emerged from this period in history as a very different place. In some countries, religious reform was accompanied by political reform. A number of European monarchs challenged age-old traditions of power in relation to the Church. They seized and then redistributed power, shifting it from the Church—and its leader, the pope—to the state. This shift in power made monarchs more powerful. Over time, new forms of government were created in which more people had a voice.

In time, the Catholic Church listened to the critics and began to reform itself from within. It became a more unified institution, despite having lost some of its political influence. To a large extent, much of northern Europe and England became a stronghold of Protestantism. However, most other western European states remained Catholic. As a result, European society was divided along religious lines in a way it had never been before. These divisions would continue to shape European history for many years to come.

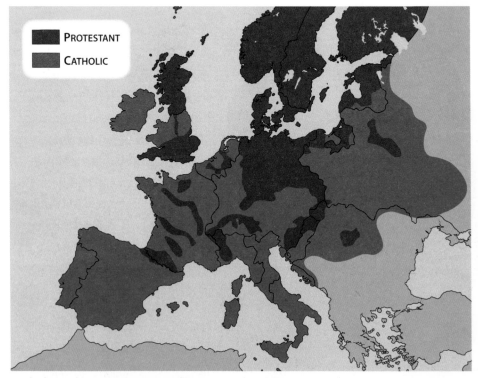

Catholic and Protestant areas of Europe in the 1500s

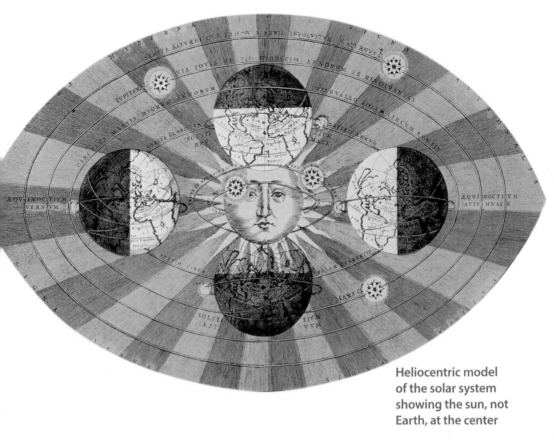

Heliocentric model of the solar system showing the sun, not Earth, at the center

Against this backdrop, scientific advances were being made. Scientists such as Nicolaus Copernicus and Galileo Galilei made discoveries that led them to reject the long-held belief that Earth lay at the center of the universe. Instead, they proposed a new view of the solar system, with the sun and not Earth at its center.

Of Princes and Protestants

When many people hear the word *Protestant*, they think about Martin Luther and other religious reformers of the Reformation. However, the word actually originated as a result of several German princes protesting a ruling by the Church that Luther be arrested and punished for his rebellious actions and ideas. These princes were the original "Protestants." Over time, however, the term came to be associated with religious reformers, like Luther, who protested against certain teachings and practices of the Church during the Reformation.

Renaissance and Rebirth

As you know, the Renaissance was a cultural movement in Europe characterized by renewed interest in ancient Greek and Roman civilization and learning. This revival of ancient ideas and ideals—the word *Renaissance*

means "rebirth"—took hold during the latter part of the Middle Ages. The Renaissance sparked enormous creativity and experimentation in European art, literature, architecture, music, and science.

The Cathedral of Florence, Italy

The Renaissance got its start in the Italian city of Florence. In time, however, the focus shifted from Florence to Rome, where the Church had its papal offices, or headquarters. From about 1450 CE onward, one pope after another decided to support great Renaissance artists and architects, just like the wealthy residents of Florence did. The popes called artists to Rome and set them to work creating some of the most magnificent paintings, sculptures, and buildings of all time.

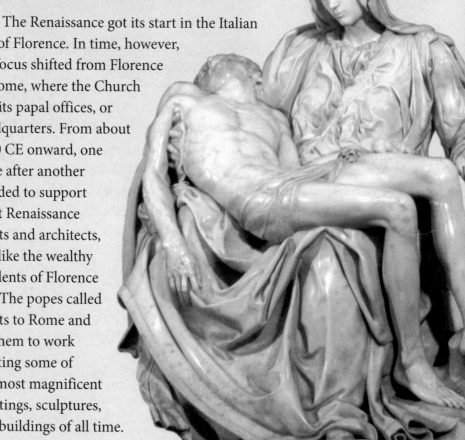

Michelangelo's *Pietà*, located in St. Peter's Basilica in Rome, 1499 C

Raphael's *The School of Athens*, located in the Apostolic Palace, 1510 CE

The popes justified these artistic undertakings by claiming that when people saw majestic buildings, gorgeous paintings, and beautiful sculptures, they would be in awe. They would ponder the glory of God. They would also appreciate the splendor and power of the Church and be thankful to be a part of it. But its power and role in people's lives was about to be seriously threatened.

Chapter 4
The Reformation Movement

THE BIG QUESTION
What did Martin Luther, John Calvin, and others contribute to the Reformation movement?

Martin Luther sparked the Reformation, a movement that brought about great religious and political changes. As a young boy growing up in Germany, he could not have known that he would be responsible for such change.

Martin Luther was born into a relatively wealthy German family. His father prospered in the copper mining business. His family had enough money to send him to good schools and eventually to the University of Erfurt, one of the best universities in Germany. Luther was an excellent student and earned two degrees. In 1505 CE, at age 21, he decided to pursue a third degree, in law. But six weeks later he had a sudden change of heart.

What happened? As Luther later told the story, he was walking home one night when a terrible storm came. Thunder boomed and lightning blazed across the sky. Suddenly a bolt of lightning struck dangerously close, knocking Luther to the ground. As the storm raged around him, the terrified Luther vowed that if he survived, he would give his life to God and become a monk.

Luther did survive. True to his promise, but much to his father's dismay, he stopped studying law and entered the Augustinian monastery in Erfurt.

Growing Doubts

Like most Christians of his time, Luther initially accepted what the Church taught—the only way into heaven was to do good works, aid the poor, confess his sins, and follow its teachings. But during the years Luther spent in the monastery at Erfurt, he had a lot of time to read the Bible. He **pondered** biblical passages—as well as his own beliefs. Like most people of this age, Luther wanted to ensure for himself a place in heaven. He began to

Luther at Erfurt by
Sir Joseph Noel
Paton, 1861

question, however, the Church's teachings with regard to what people had to do to make that happen. He also questioned the role of priests in people's lives. His views were a direct challenge to the Church in Rome.

Luther's Ninety-Five Theses

After several years, Luther was transferred from Erfurt to a monastery at Wittenberg. There Luther attended the University of Wittenberg. He earned an advanced degree in biblical **theology** and became a teacher at the university.

Luther was a gifted teacher and a powerful speaker. As he continued teaching, he struggled to come to a clearer understanding of his own beliefs and how they differed from Church teachings. He was angered by practices within the Church that he thought were corrupt. In 1517 CE, an event took place that changed Luther's life and ultimately European history.

If you recall, the Church raised money by issuing indulgences. People believed that indulgences could speed up their journey to heaven, and shorten the amount of time they spent in purgatory, a place people believed their souls went before reaching heaven.

The practice of issuing indulgences in exchange for money became intolerable for Luther when he heard about a Dominican friar named John Tetzel. Tetzel not only issued indulgences, he proclaimed that as soon as a coin was received by the Church, a soul was released from purgatory. It was essentially saying you could buy the way of a soul into heaven.

Outraged, Luther decided to act. He composed a list of 95 objections to the practice of issuing indulgences and sent it in a letter to his **superiors**. In addition, on October 31, 1517 CE, Luther nailed a copy of this list, later called his Ninety-Five **Theses**, to the door of the church at the University of Wittenberg. This action was an open invitation to discuss and debate his point of view.

Martin Luther nails the
Ninety-Five Theses to the church door.

Another Storm Brewing

Luther was trying to start a discussion with his theses, not a revolution. But people who were unhappy with the Church were energized by Luther's actions. Luther's theses were quickly translated from Latin into German and—thanks to the printing press—thousands of copies were distributed across Europe in just a few months.

Encouraged, Luther began speaking out more openly against other Church teachings. He also wrote essays in which he discussed the importance of faith and the fact that all believers, wealthy or poor, were equal. These writings, including *On Christian Liberty, On the Freedom of a Christian [Man]*, and *An Open Letter to the Christian Nobility of the German Nation*, were also translated, printed, and widely distributed across Europe.

As you can imagine, not everyone was pleased about the stir Luther was causing. In 1518 CE, the pope summoned Luther to Rome to explain his actions. Fortunately for Luther, Frederick III, the elector, or ruler, of Saxony, **intervened**.

Frederick was in a tricky position. He had received a letter from the pope urging him to turn Luther over to Church officials in Rome. Frederick didn't necessarily agree with Luther's ideas on religion. However, as ruler of the region in which Luther lived, he didn't like the pope telling his subjects what to do, either. In fact, Frederick wanted to increase the power of the German nobility. Not only that, he was tired of sending German money to Rome to pay for perceived papal **extravagance**. He also suspected that Luther, a German, would not be treated fairly in Rome.

Instead of sending Luther to Rome, Frederick had his hearing moved to a city in southern Germany. There, Luther was questioned by Church officials about his beliefs. He refused to change his mind.

Luther's refusal to back down made the pope even angrier. In 1520 CE, the pope issued an official document called a papal bull. In his bull, the pope attacked Luther and said his writings were those of a heretic. Luther was ordered to recant, or take back, all that he'd said about the Church and its teachings.

A Papal What?

Important orders issued by the pope were written on parchment and sealed with a lump of lead. To make the document official, the pope pressed his signet ring into the lump of metal while it was still warm and soft. The lead lump was called a *bulla* in Latin, which is why these papal documents came to be called *bulls*.

How did Luther respond? On December 10, 1520 CE, students, professors, and some of the townspeople of Wittenberg gathered before a blazing bonfire. They watched as Martin Luther defiantly dropped a copy of the papal bull into the blaze. In doing so, Luther was publicly **defying** the pope. It was a bold and dangerous move. A month later, the pope formally labeled Luther a heretic and excommunicated him from the Church.

Luther Burning the Papal Bull by Freidrich Paul Thumann, 1872

Refusal and Refuge

Many Germans, including some German noblemen, did not think Luther had been given a fair hearing. In 1521 CE, Luther was ordered to appear before a special assembly, called a diet, in the German city of Worms. The Diet of Worms included knights, Church officials, and representatives from various towns and regions. When Luther arrived, he thought he would get a chance to defend his ideas. Instead, Church officials piled his writings in front of him and again ordered him to denounce his ideas. Luther refused.

The Diet of Worms declared Luther to be not just a heretic, but also a criminal. Since it was common to kill heretics and criminals, Luther's life was in danger. Once again, Frederick III of Saxony came to his aid.

As Luther traveled back to Wittenberg, the elector arranged for masked horsemen to pretend to kidnap Luther. Frederick did not believe Luther was guilty of any crime that warranted death. He was also well aware that Luther had gained the support of many of Frederick's own subjects. Luther was whisked off to a castle where he remained in hiding and under Frederick's protection for 10 months. During that time Luther began translating the New Testament into German, setting a style of language that was more accessible to people.

By the time Luther came out of hiding, his push for **reform** had turned into a religious and political movement that had been greatly strengthened. The power of the printing press was evident as his ideas and beliefs spread far and wide. Those people who believed in his ideas left the Catholic Church and began to worship according to Luther's teachings.

Martin Luther before the Diet of Worms by Wolfgang Taubert

Luther and Erasmus

Martin Luther continued to write about his religious ideas for the rest of his life. In the 1520s, he got into a debate with Desiderius Erasmus, a Dutch Renaissance humanist and scholar. (Renaissance humanists emphasized learning and scholarship and the ability of human beings to figure out for themselves what is true and important in life.) Like Luther, Erasmus wanted to see reform in the Catholic Church. Unlike Luther, he did not break away from the Church and respected many of its teachings and traditions.

In their writings, the two men debated many topics, including what free will was and whether human beings have it. Were people free to choose to be good, or not?

Erasmus

Other Protestant Reformers

Martin Luther set the Reformation in motion. Other religious reformers soon followed. Each reformer had his own ideas and his own vision of reform. Each gained his own set of followers. Disputes, even fighting, arose between some of these groups.

One radical **sect**, labeled Anabaptists by those who viewed them negatively, took control of the city of Münster, Germany, in 1534 CE. This sect established an independent community, or commune of believers. They set themselves apart from the world that existed outside the city walls. A Dutch tailor declared himself "king" of the community. In some ways they were social rebels, challenging the social order. The Münster Rebellion, as it was later known, didn't last much more than a year. The Anabaptists were either executed or forced out of the city. But it was a sign of how the

Reformation was changing not only people's religious beliefs, but their ideas about politics and governments, too.

One of the most influential religious reformers in addition to Luther was a Frenchman named John Calvin. Calvin settled in Switzerland, in the city of Geneva. His ideas and teachings attracted many followers, and soon Geneva became the center of the religious reform movement known as Calvinism.

Calvin was opposed to many of the traditions and teachings of the Catholic Church. He believed that if the Bible did not specifically tell you to do something in a church service, then you shouldn't do it. He also believed in "predestination." This is the belief that some people have already been chosen by God for salvation. Those chosen, said Calvin, would lead a simple, **self-disciplined** life, devoted to God. Calvinist churches were very plain and bare, with no stained-glass windows, no statues of saints, and no paintings.

Calvin also stressed social reform. He worked for better hospitals and special care for the poor and needy. He also started a school called the Geneva Academy. Graduates of the academy traveled to many countries, including France, the Netherlands, Scotland, and England, where they spread Calvinist beliefs to new groups. In England, one such group was the Puritans. They brought Calvin's ideas with them when they journeyed to New England in the early 1600s and established the Massachusetts Bay Colony.

John Calvin

Chapter 5
What Is at the Center of the Universe?

THE BIG QUESTION
What new scientific theories were proposed by Nicolaus Copernicus, Johannes Kepler, and Galileo Galilei, and how did the Church respond?

You've probably seen the sun rise and set many times. You've noticed how it slowly moves across the sky during the day. Well, at least it seems to move. If you've paid attention during science, you know that the sun doesn't orbit Earth. Earth orbits, or travels around, the sun, as do the other planets in our solar system. Earth also spins as it orbits the sun. It's because Earth is spinning that the sun appears to move across the sky every day.

But imagine not knowing any of that. Imagine trying to explain the relationship between the earth and the sun based only on what you could see by looking up at the sky. If you think about it that way, it's easy to understand why people in centuries past arrived at other conclusions.

The idea that the earth is at the center of things is called the geocentric model of the universe. At the beginning of the Reformation, this is what almost everyone in Europe believed to be true. The Catholic Church also supported this geocentric view.

But the Reformation was a time when many people were questioning long-held beliefs. Martin Luther and other Protestant reformers were challenging religious beliefs. Scientifically minded reformers were looking hard at the geocentric model of the universe, and they were discovering that it, too, needed to be challenged.

Systema
TIVS CREATI
THE SI
CANA IN
EXHIBITVM

45

From Earth-Centered to Sun-Centered: Ptolemy and Copernicus

The idea that the earth was at the center of the universe seems to have had its start in ancient Greece. The Greek philosopher Aristotle wrote about it as early as the fourth century BCE. During the second century CE, a Greek astronomer and mathematician named Claudius Ptolemy expanded on Aristotle's ideas. In fact, the geocentric model is sometimes called the Ptolemaic model.

Ptolemy supported Aristotle's view that Earth stood still at the center of the universe, while the sun, moon, and planets all revolved around it. He thought these heavenly bodies were located in different spheres—something like gigantic, crystal-clear bubbles—with the bigger spheres around the smaller spheres, and Earth at the very center. For many hundreds of years, people accepted Ptolemy's model of the universe. No one questioned his views—no one, that is, until a Polish astronomer named Nicolaus Copernicus came along.

Ptolemy's geocentric model

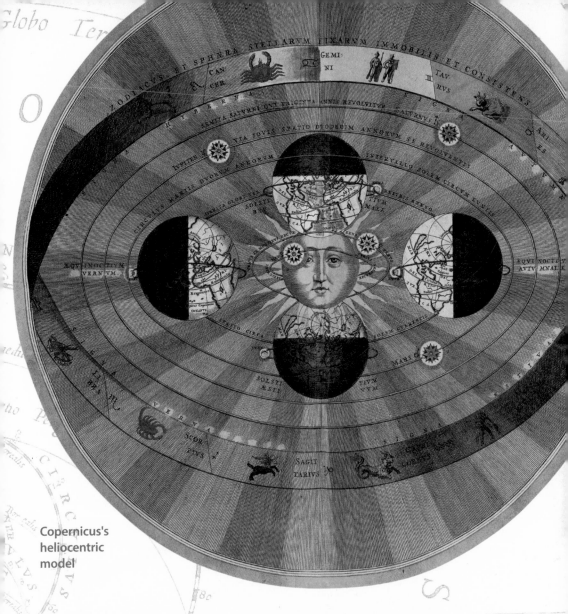

Copernicus's heliocentric model

Copernicus was born in 1473 CE, in the Polish city of Thorn (now called Toruń). In the early 1500s—about the time Martin Luther was forming his religious beliefs—Copernicus was studying the movements of the planets and stars. (He made all his observations with the naked eye, because the telescope hadn't been invented.) What Copernicus observed happening in the heavens, however, didn't really match Ptolemy's geocentric model. He concluded that Ptolemy and the ancients were wrong. Earth does not sit still at the center of the universe. Instead, Earth and other planets revolve around the sun! Copernicus's findings supported a heliocentric, rather than a geocentric, view of the universe.

Copernicus had made a great discovery. But he did not run out and shout it from the rooftops. In fact, he kept quiet about his work. Why? For one thing, he did not have enough evidence to prove his ideas beyond all doubt. Copernicus may also have feared what would happen to him if he publicly **contradicted** the Church's beliefs about the nature of the universe and the earth's place in it.

It wasn't until 1543 CE, at the very end of his life, that Copernicus published his findings in a book called *On the Revolutions of the Celestial Spheres*. According to some accounts, Copernicus was handed the first printed copy of his book while on his deathbed. Once again the power of printing helped to spread new ideas, this time in the area of science.

Initially, Copernicus's heliocentric model did not get much attention or cause much disturbance. But a handful of European astronomers believed that Copernicus was on to something.

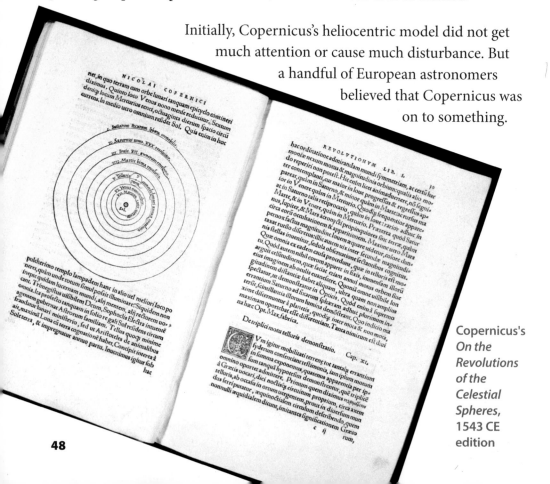

Copernicus's *On the Revolutions of the Celestial Spheres*, 1543 CE edition

Johannes Kepler

German mathematician and astronomer Johannes Kepler was one of these people. While studying at the University of Tübingen in the 1590s, Kepler's mathematics professor introduced him to Copernicus's heliocentric theory. Being a mathematician, Kepler was able to understand and appreciate Copernicus's observations and calculations. Over the next few years, Kepler pursued his own studies of the night sky, eventually publishing a book, *Misterium Cosmographicum* or *The Cosmographic Mystery*. In this book he presented a mathematical model that explained the relative distances of the planets from the sun based on his—and Copernicus's—observations.

Johannes Kepler

Kepler's book impressed another astronomer, Tycho Brahe. In 1600 CE, Brahe invited Kepler to come to Prague to help him calculate planetary orbits. Within a year, Brahe died and Kepler took over the work. Kepler continued his astronomical observations and eventually formulated **theories** about the way the different planets orbit the sun. These theories later came to be called Kepler's laws of planetary motion.

Most of Kepler's **contemporaries** had not changed their thinking, which is why Kepler was so excited when he learned about the discoveries of Italian astronomer Galileo Galilei.

Kepler's diagram of planetary orbits from his work *Epitome Astronomiae Copernicanae*, published between 1617–1621 CE

49

Galileo and the Telescope

Born in Pisa, Italy, in 1564 CE, Galileo Galilei (many people refer to him just by his first name, Galileo) started his career thinking he might become a doctor. At the age of 17, Galileo headed off to the University of Pisa with that plan in mind. But after only a couple of years, he left medical school to study—and then later teach—mathematics.

Galileo was a brilliant mathematician. He made many calculations and discoveries about how objects move. As a well-educated man, he was very familiar with the writings of Aristotle and Ptolemy and the geocentric model of the universe. But he had also read Copernicus's book. Like Copernicus, however, Galileo recognized that no one had yet found conclusive proof that Earth and the other planets orbited the sun. At the time, Galileo was more interested in explaining how things worked on Earth, rather than out in space. But within a few years, his interests changed, thanks to a new invention.

In 1608 CE, a Dutch glassmaker named Hans Lippershey constructed one of the first telescopes. Galileo learned about the invention and very quickly improved on the design. Within a year, he was using a telescope to scan the night sky. He saw much that directly contradicted the ideas of Aristotle and Ptolemy. These ancient scholars had believed that all heavenly bodies were perfect, with smooth, unmarked surfaces. But through his telescope, Galileo saw that the moon's surface was rough and uneven, marked with mountains, valleys, and craters. Aristotle and Ptolemy also believed the knowledge of the heavens was complete; in other words, what they could see was what existed. With his telescope, Galileo discovered four new moons orbiting Jupiter.

In 1610 CE, Galileo published a book, *Sidereus Nuncius*, or *The Starry Messenger*, in which he described what

Portrait of Galileo Galilei by Justus Sustermans, 1636 CE

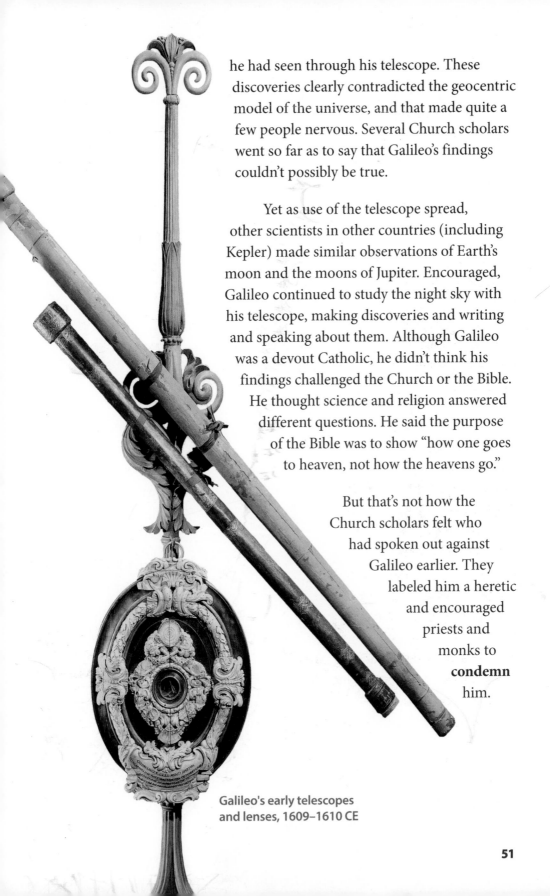

he had seen through his telescope. These discoveries clearly contradicted the geocentric model of the universe, and that made quite a few people nervous. Several Church scholars went so far as to say that Galileo's findings couldn't possibly be true.

Yet as use of the telescope spread, other scientists in other countries (including Kepler) made similar observations of Earth's moon and the moons of Jupiter. Encouraged, Galileo continued to study the night sky with his telescope, making discoveries and writing and speaking about them. Although Galileo was a devout Catholic, he didn't think his findings challenged the Church or the Bible. He thought science and religion answered different questions. He said the purpose of the Bible was to show "how one goes to heaven, not how the heavens go."

But that's not how the Church scholars felt who had spoken out against Galileo earlier. They labeled him a heretic and encouraged priests and monks to **condemn** him.

Galileo's early telescopes and lenses, 1609–1610 CE

Galileo before the Inquistion by Robert Fleury, 1847

Soon, much more powerful members of the Church began to speak against Galileo as well. Galileo wrote letters and gave speeches in order to defend himself, his findings, and Copernicus's views, but things only got worse.

Almost Silenced

In 1615 CE, the Inquisition, or the court of the Catholic Church, discussed Galileo and the ideas of Copernicus for over two months. The judges, called inquisitors, decided that Copernicus's ideas went against Church teachings. They ordered Galileo to stop promoting the idea that the earth moves rather than the sun. Galileo realized that he risked imprisonment, or worse, if he continued. Keeping quiet was much safer —and would also enable him to continue working in private.

Galileo decided to keep quiet, and did so for several years. However, when a new pope, Urban VIII, came into power, Galileo hoped that this new man with new ideas would listen to him. In 1624 CE, Galileo asked the pope for permission to write a book that would discuss the ocean tides in relation to the contrasting ideas of Ptolemy and Copernicus. The pope gave Galileo permission to write the book—as long as he treated the ideas of Copernicus as **speculation**, not as truth.

Galileo wrote the book as he wanted to, titling it *Dialogue Concerning the Two Chief World Systems*. The Inquisition was not pleased. Galileo was summoned to Rome to stand trial and was accused of being a heretic. In order to spare himself punishment, and possible execution, Galileo eventually recanted. But astronomers and mathematicians who came after him found more and more evidence that Galileo, Kepler, and Copernicus were correct. Around the middle of the 1700s, the Church began to change its position, acknowledging the huge body of evidence supporting motion of the planets around the sun.

Chapter 6

The Catholic Church Responds

THE BIG QUESTION
How did the Catholic Church respond to the Protestant Reformation movement?

In the early 1500s, probably no one—not even Martin Luther—imagined how much Europe would change as a result of the Reformation. But as the religious reform movement gained strength, many people left the Catholic Church and **embraced** the teachings of various Protestant reformers.

Before Luther wrote his Ninety-Five Theses, western Europe had been largely united by a single religion: Catholicism. After Luther, northern and northwestern Europe became strongholds for Lutheran, Calvinist, and other Protestant believers. Southern Europeans, especially those in Spain, France, and Italy, remained primarily Catholic. By the 1530s, Europe was deeply divided by religion.

As the number of **converts** to Protestantism grew, leaders in the Catholic Church realized they needed to take action. The Catholic Church's response to the Reformation is called the Catholic Reformation, or the Counter-Reformation. It opposed, or countered, the Protestant-driven Reformation.

Several popes were involved with the Catholic Reformation, but the man who started things moving was Pope Paul III.

The Catholic Reformation Gets Underway

In 1536 CE, Pope Paul III appointed a group of **cardinals** to investigate what was right—and wrong—with the Church. The cardinals identified many problems. These included corrupt practices such as issuing indulgences for money. Their findings also revealed a relatively uneducated priesthood, and monasteries and religious **orders** that were not following Church teachings.

After considering the cardinals' report, the pope and his advisors laid down plans for reform. They decided to focus on weeding out corrupt practices within the Church. They saw the need to more clearly state Catholic beliefs and teachings. They also hoped to halt the spread of Protestantism and bring former Catholics back into the faith.

The goals seemed clear. Now the challenge was to accomplish them.

Ignatius of Loyola and the Jesuits

One of the first things Pope Paul III did was to encourage new religious orders within the Church to help promote reform. Perhaps the most influential of these Catholic organizations was the Society of Jesus, or the Jesuits, as they were also known. Ignatius of Loyola, a Spanish priest, had founded the Jesuits several years earlier.

Ignatius as a soldier at the Battle of Pamplona in 1521 CE

Ignatius had taken a long and unusual path to the priesthood. Born in 1491 CE—the year before Christopher Columbus sailed for the New World—he had spent his early adult years in the Spanish military. While defending a Spanish fort from an invading French army, Ignatius was hit by a cannonball. The cannonball shattered the bones in one of his legs. His recovery was slow and painful. He was forced to spend a lot of time lying down while his leg healed. To pass the days, Ignatius read. However, the only available reading materials in the place where he was recovering were religious books. There was an illustrated book that told the story of Christ's life and a book about Catholic saints.

As Ignatius read, he felt he was being called by God to a new life of good works. After his leg healed, he left the military and studied to become a priest.

While studying for the priesthood, Ignatius kept detailed journals in which he wrote about the challenges of his new **calling**. Later in life, he turned his journals into an inspirational text called *Spiritual Exercises*, complete with prayers and meditations. Ignatius thought the book might help guide others on their own **spiritual** journeys. *Spiritual Exercises* became quite popular and was translated into many different languages.

Ignatius was elected the first leader of the Society of Jesus, after it officially became a Catholic religious order. He counseled his fellow Jesuits to serve "without hard words or contempt for people's errors." Ignatius died in 1556 CE. He was declared a saint by the Catholic Church in the early 1600s, and so became St. Ignatius of Loyola.

Ignatius of Loyola

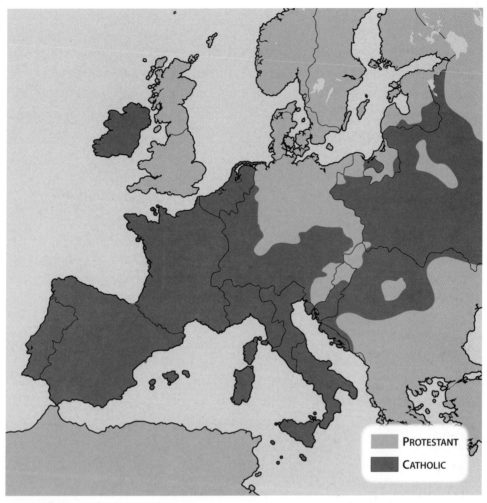

Ireland and southern European countries remained primarily Catholic.

How did the Jesuits help the Catholic Reformation? They worked to revive Catholicism in Europe and spread the faith to the New World. The members of the Jesuit order were well-educated. They were dedicated to teaching as well as preaching, and they built many schools and universities. Jesuits became tutors to the children of princes and noblemen in many European countries. Jesuits traveled far and wide as missionaries, bringing education and Catholic beliefs to the Americas and parts of Asia. Although the Catholic Church had lost power and influence in Europe during the Reformation, the Jesuits helped the Church regain some of what had been lost. They also helped the Church grow in parts of the world beyond Europe.

Council of Trent

In 1545 CE, Pope Paul III sent out a papal bull summoning the Catholic bishops of Europe to Trento, a city in what is now northern Italy. There they met to discuss and decide how best to reform the Church. The Council of Trent, as it came to be called, was the Catholic Church's organized response to the Reformation.

The Council of Trent met in three separate sessions between 1545 and 1563 CE. The Council issued formal declarations that explained why the Church disagreed with the teachings of Protestant reformers. They clarified the doctrines that formed the basis of the Catholic faith. They affirmed that Church traditions as well as the Bible were the foundation of Catholic beliefs. The Council also took steps to reform corrupt practices within the Church by issuing a number of reform **decrees**.

Decisions made by the Council played a key role in **revitalizing** and unifying the Catholic Church. Some parts of Europe that had turned to Protestantism, including Austria, Poland, and a part of Germany called Bavaria, reverted back to Catholicism.

Other Actions of the Council

In Chapter One, you read about Johann Gutenberg and the invention of a printing press. By the early 1500s, hundreds of thousands of books and pamphlets were in print and being read by Europeans. Leaders of the Catholic Church recognized the power of the printed word. In an attempt to stop the spread of anti-Catholic writings, the Council of Trent decided to try to control what Catholics were allowed to read. The Council had Church leaders review new publications. If those materials went against Church teachings, they were **censored**.

Burning of heretical books by Pedro Berruguete

Furthermore, the Council created the *Index of Forbidden Books*, a list of publications that were banned, or forbidden. By creating the index, the Church hoped to keep heretical or what they considered **immoral** writings from corrupting the minds of its faithful followers. Nearly all books written by Protestants were banned. Even the writings of some reform-minded Catholics, such as Desiderius Erasmus, were banned as well. Anyone caught reading, selling, or owning a banned book faced punishment.

Pope Paul III also revived the Inquisition as part of the Church's response to the Reformation. As you have discovered, the Inquisition was the court system of the Catholic Church. It was tasked with rooting out heresy. The *Index of Forbidden Books* and the Inquisition were the two primary tools that the Church used to counteract Protestant ideas.

Results of the Reformations

By the second half of the 1500s, many of the problems in the Catholic Church that had triggered the Reformation had been corrected or greatly reduced. The Council of Trent had purged the Church, leaving it stronger and more united. However, it was clear that Catholic and Protestant sects, though now reconciled on some issues, would never be united again.

The Reformation and the Catholic Reformation left Christians in Europe bitterly divided. In Catholic-controlled areas, Protestants were **persecuted** as heretics. In Protestant strongholds, Catholics were persecuted with equal brutality. Some conflicts flared into terrible wars that lasted many years. In fact, these two religious reformations sparked many years of warfare in Europe.

But there also were positive outcomes as a result of these two reform movements. Ordinary people—not just the wealthy nobility—had access to Bibles and other texts that were printed in their native language. To some extent, people had a choice about which religion they could follow. They were able to associate more freely with others who shared the same beliefs. Kings gained greater control over their kingdoms. And over time, their subjects began to identify more with countries and empires rather than with a particular religion.

Erasmus and the Reformation

"When I get a little money, I buy books; if any is left I buy food and clothes."

Did that quotation make you chuckle? Did it also make you think? Could books and learning be more important than what a person eats or wears? A man named Desiderius Erasmus of Rotterdam (1466–1536 CE) penned that quotation around 1500 CE. The statement is typical of Erasmus. He spent his life writing books and essays that often seemed funny at first glance. Yet they expressed ideas that challenged readers to think deeply about serious subjects.

Erasmus was a Dutch theologian and scholar with a tremendous talent for writing about important subjects related to society and religion. Erasmus played an important role in the Reformation.

Monk Turned Scholar

Erasmus was born in Rotterdam, Netherlands. His early education began in monastic schools, where it was assumed he would grow up to become a monk. In his early twenties, Erasmus took the vows necessary to become a monk and soon after was admitted to the Catholic priesthood. However, monastic life didn't suit him. He left after only a few years to begin a career doing what he loved most: learning, reading, and writing.

Erasmus pored over the works of ancient scholars from Greece and Rome as well as the writings of contemporary thinkers. He traveled widely and became acquainted with intellectuals throughout Europe. He was a keen observer and soon devoted himself to writing about the problems of his day. At the beginning of the 1500s, many of those problems had to do with the Catholic Church.

Portrait of Erasmus by Hans Holbein, 1523 CE

Erasmus was a devout Catholic and respected the Catholic faith. But he was dismayed by the corruption and abusive use of power he saw among some Church leaders. Erasmus's goal was to use the power of the written word to stimulate Church reform. In his writings, he urged Catholics to more closely follow the examples and teachings of Jesus. He stressed focusing less on rituals and ceremonies and more on the religious meaning behind them. He felt that Christians should not obey Church leaders blindly. Instead, they should study Jesus's life and teachings by reading the Bible themselves.

By advocating these ideas, Erasmus paved the way for Luther and other Protestant reformers. Unlike Luther and those who followed him, however, Erasmus never tried to break away from the Catholic Church. He hoped to improve it from within—peacefully and thoughtfully.

A New Bible

Erasmus wanted words to promote religious reform. It seems fitting that one of his greatest contributions to the Reformation was his translation of the New Testament.

For more than a thousand years, the Church had been using what was called the *Vulgate Bible*. It had been written during the 300s in Latin by a scholar named Eusebius Hieronymus, or St. Jerome as he was later known. In Jerome's day, there were many versions of the Bible circulating in the Christian world. Some were quite different from others. Jerome was tasked by the pope with producing one, standardized, Latin Bible to help support a universal Church doctrine. Jerome used ancient Latin, Greek, and Hebrew manuscripts to produce his Latin translation of the Bible.

During the early 1500s, Erasmus studied the original Greek manuscripts on which the *Vulgate Bible* was based. He discovered that Jerome's translation had flaws. Erasmus wanted to correct the errors. Around 1514 CE, Erasmus moved to Basel (now in Switzerland but then part of the German empire), which had become a hub for printing. Basel was home to some of the best printing presses and book publishers in Europe. Erasmus had been working on a new Greek translation of the New Testament, based on original manuscripts. In 1516 CE, he published a New Testament that was unlike anything Christians had seen before. On each page, one column had the text in Greek, while the second column was in Latin. The basis for the Latin text was the *Vulgate Bible*, but Erasmus had edited it to more closely match the meaning of the original Greek manuscripts.

Erasmus's New Testament was the product of the most scholarly study of the Bible that anyone had ever undertaken in Europe. He published a second edition in 1519 CE in which the Latin text was largely his own elegant translation. Erasmus's New Testament became immensely popular in Europe and made him famous. The Catholic Church embraced it; it didn't hurt that Erasmus dedicated the first edition to Pope Leo X! Along with some of Erasmus's other writings, his New Testament also served as a source of inspiration for the first Protestant reformer: Martin Luther.

Other Translations of the Bible

Martin Luther thought Erasmus's New Testament was wonderful. Luther used it as the primary source for his translation of the New Testament into German. A few years later, William Tyndale used it as the basis for his translation of the New Testament into English.

Copy of Tyndale's Bible, based on Erasmus's translation, 1535 CE

Caught in the Middle

After the publication of his New Testament, Erasmus became one of the most widely known and influential scholars in western Europe. At roughly the same time, Martin Luther's outspoken criticisms of the Church set the Reformation in motion. As the movement spread, Luther and his supporters called on Erasmus to join their cause. They had read Erasmus's criticisms of the Church, and his writings that urged Christians to more closely follow Christ's biblical teachings. The religious reformers assumed that Erasmus would support them in their break with the Church.

But he didn't. Erasmus preferred not to take sides in the conflict he could see was developing. He declined Luther's repeated requests that he openly join the reformers' cause. He thought Luther's break from the Church could only lead to trouble.

The more Luther insisted, the more firmly Erasmus refused. The two men never met face-to-face to discuss the matter. Instead, they sent letters to each other and to others involved in the debate. Throughout these written exchanges, Erasmus remained polite. He wrote about Luther: "...I shall not write against him...I have taught well nigh all that Luther teaches, only less violently....I hope that all the tumult Luther has stirred up will, like a drastic medicine, somehow bring about the health of the Church."

Luther wasn't nearly as kind when expressing his opinion of Erasmus. In a letter to another reformer he wrote: "[Erasmus] might have been of great service...[but]...he is the worst **foe** of Christ that has arisen in the last thousand years."

When it became known that Erasmus wouldn't join with the Protestants, many Catholics tried to claim him as their champion instead. Several Catholic scholars and Church leaders demanded that Erasmus denounce Luther. They insisted that he make it clear that he favored Catholic doctrines over Protestant teachings. Again, Erasmus refused to take sides. This made the Catholics angry. They claimed Erasmus was being disloyal to his faith.

Erasmus was caught in the middle of the Protestant-Catholic controversy. He realized that, to some degree, his writings about Church reform had helped start the Reformation. When Catholics accused Erasmus of having "laid the egg that Luther hatched," he admitted they were partially correct. But he added that he "had expected quite another kind of bird" to hatch from that egg. In other words, although he agreed with some of Luther's ideas and teachings, he thought others were too extreme.

Growing Divisions

Erasmus could sense the tensions rising on both sides in the Reformation. He abhorred violence. As the reform movement gained momentum, Erasmus was saddened to see its religious discussions and debates turn into persecution, angry division, and bitter conflicts. Over the next few years, he did his best to stay out of the way.

When Protestants took control of Basel's city government in 1529 CE, Erasmus felt morally obligated to leave. He objected to living where Catholic worship was now legally—and forcefully—suppressed. Furthermore, Erasmus had always said his quarrel was not with the Catholic Church itself, but only with corruption and practices he felt were wrong. He remained faithful to the Catholic Church throughout his life.

Erasmus took up residence in a German town that was not in danger of being taken over by Protestants. He continued to write, but his works were widely criticized by both Catholics and Protestants, because he still refused to denounce one side over the other. Some of Erasmus's last writings **advocated** mutual tolerance between Catholics and Protestants. Neither side paid much attention to him.

In 1535 CE, Erasmus was putting the final touches on what would be the last edition of his famous New Testament. Despite the fact that Basel was still a Protestant city, he moved back there to be closer to his publisher. Although very ill, he wanted to oversee the printing of one of his life's greatest achievements.

Erasmus died in July 1556 CE. He left behind quite a large sum of money (he had sold a lot of books!). Some of it was used to publish a collection of his writings—nine large volumes in all. The rest Erasmus had requested go to providing support for girls from poor families and students at the University of Basel.

Looking Out for Luther

Luther's words against Erasmus seem awfully harsh, considering that when Luther was labeled a heretic by the Church, Erasmus took steps that likely saved Luther's life. Erasmus wrote to Frederick III of Saxony, the German elector who ruled over the region where Luther lived. In the letter, Erasmus said that, in his opinion, Luther was not a heretic. He urged Frederick to protect Luther and make sure he didn't fall into the hands of his enemies, for they would likely kill him. Frederick took Erasmus's advice, and made sure that Luther remained safe. Luther knew about the letter.

Frederick III by Lucas Cranach the Elder, 1525 CE

Life and Achievements of Copernicus

Nicolaus Copernicus accomplished quite a feat in the mid-1500s: he made the earth and the sun change places! He didn't physically give them a push, of course. But he was the first European to propose that the sun, rather than the earth, was at the center of the solar system. Although it may not seem like such a **radical** idea today, it was an enormous change in the view of the universe and the earth's place within it.

The Polish Astronomer

Copernicus's father, a well-to-do merchant, died when Copernicus was 10 years old. Fortunately, his uncle stepped in to take care of the family and help Copernicus get a good education. At age 18, he headed off to the University of Krakow where he studied many subjects, including mathematics and astronomy.

In his astronomy classes, Copernicus learned all about Aristotle's and Ptolemy's geocentric models of the universe. Everyone at the time had grown up with this view. On the surface, it seemed to make sense.

The Latin Name Game

If you could zip back to the 1500s to look at Copernicus' birth certificate, you might find it a little confusing. Instead of Nicolaus Copernicus, the name on the document was "Mikolaj Kopernik"! In Copernicus's day, it was common for scholars to "Latinize" their names. They changed the spelling so their names looked and sounded more like Latin words. Mikolaj Kopernik became Nicolaus Copernicus sometime during his university studies.

Aristotle had also stated that heavy objects naturally fall toward the center of the universe. The fact that you could pick up a stone, let go, and watch it fall to the ground was thought to be **proof** that the earth was at the universe's heart.

Copernicus continued his education in Italy, spending another 10 years or so studying medicine and law at several Italian universities. During part of his stay in Italy, he rented rooms from an astronomy professor named Domenico Maria Novara. Novara questioned the geocentric model of the solar system, and he may have prompted Copernicus's thinking that perhaps the ancient beliefs weren't entirely correct. For some time, Copernicus had been making his own astronomical observations. In 1500 CE, for example, he witnessed a lunar eclipse in Rome.

Copernicus viewing eclipse in Rome by J. Presno

Copernicus on the tower in Frombork, Jan Matejko, 1800s

When Copernicus finally returned to Poland around 1503 CE, he eventually settled in Frauenburg (now Frombork), where he worked as a physician, lawyer, and church administrator. Despite his busy life, he made time for astronomy. He set up a small observatory for observing the stars in a tower that was part of the wall surrounding the town. Copernicus made all of his observations of the night sky with the naked eye (his eyesight must have been very good!). It's not hard to imagine him working alone in the middle of the night, squinting up at the stars and making mathematical calculations.

Over time, Copernicus observed that the planets moved in ways that didn't agree with the long-held geocentric model. The old model simply didn't explain the facts. Copernicus began to formulate a theory that differed profoundly from the ideas of Aristotle and Ptolemy. It also contradicted the Earth-centered view of the world supported by the Catholic Church and many Protestants.

The Little Commentary

Sometime between 1510 and 1514 CE, Copernicus sent handwritten copies of a booklet he had put together to several astronomers and philosophers he knew. In very brief terms, the booklet outlined his new heliocentric theory. It put the sun, not the earth, at the center of the universe. Titled *Commentariolus*, or *The Little Commentary*, the booklet listed seven fundamental conclusions that Copernicus had reached, based on his observations of the night sky.

- *Heavenly bodies (objects) do not all revolve around a single point.*

- *The center of the earth is not the center of the universe.*

- *All the spheres (planets) rotate around the sun, which is near the center of the universe.*

- *The distance from the earth to the stars is far greater than the distance from the earth to the sun.*

- *Stars seem to move across the night sky because Earth is rotating.*

- *The sun's position in the sky changes throughout the year because Earth is changing position as it revolves around the sun.*

- *Some of the planets seem at times to move backward in their orbits because of the way we are seeing them from our viewpoint here on Earth.*

In just a few pages, Copernicus summarized what was a radical new theory. He also added a comment that suggested he was working on a much larger, more complete book about it. The book would, he promised, contain the mathematical proofs to support his ideas and conclusions about the heavens. The only problem was that nearly 30 years passed before the world got to see it.

A Life's Work

Copernicus observed the heavens night after night, month after month, year after year. He recorded details about when and how the planets and stars moved. He made complex mathematical calculations, geometrical drawings, and tables of figures. He worked out exactly how long it took for different planets to orbit the sun. He collected enormous amounts of data, because he wanted his life's greatest work to be as accurate as possible.

Copernicus's great work was a book titled *De Revolutionibus Orbium Coelestium*, which translates as *On the Revolutions of the Celestial Orbs*. The book was made up of six sections, each focused on a different part of Copernicus's research. Together, they laid out his theory of the universe in which all the planets, including the earth, orbit the sun.

No one knows exactly when Copernicus finished writing *On the Revolutions*. What is known is that he waited a very long time to publish it. As a Catholic, Copernicus may have been wary of the Church's reaction to his radical new view. However, some historians think it is more likely that he just kept adding to it, making more observations and doing more calculations. Copernicus also lived in a rather remote part of Poland, and Frauenburg was a very small town. He was a bit of a hermit who didn't travel much and didn't interact with many other scientists and scholars. He was also far from places where there were large printing presses. *On the Revolutions* might never have been published at all if it hadn't been for a young German named Georg Rheticus.

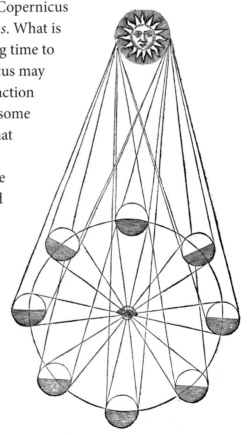

Diagram from *De Revolutionibus Orbium Coelestium*

Rheticus was a professor of mathematics and astronomy at the University of Wittenberg in Germany. He came to study with Copernicus in 1539 CE, bearing gifts in the form of new books on mathematics. The books had been printed in Germany on some of the finest presses in Europe. When Rheticus read what Copernicus had been working on for so many years, he was tremendously excited. He urged Copernicus to have it printed. Although it took more than two years, Rheticus finally convinced Copernicus to do it. In the summer of 1541 CE, Copernicus put the finishing touches on the manuscript for *On the Revolutions*. Rheticus took it to the German city of Nuremberg, where he turned it over to the best printer in town.

The Truth Comes Out

Copernicus was a devout Catholic, and Frauenburg was a Catholic town. Rheticus was a Protestant. (Remember that it was at the University of Wittenberg that Martin Luther nailed his Ninety-Five Theses to the church door.) Rheticus was probably taking a risk coming to Frauenburg, considering how much tension there was between Protestants and Catholics in many parts of Europe during the Reformation. Yet the difference in religion didn't seem to matter to Copernicus and Rheticus. They were united by their shared interest in astronomy and mathematics. Rheticus wrote about his visit to Copernicus: "I heard of the fame of Master Nicolaus Copernicus in the northern lands, and...I did not think that I should be content until I had learned something more through the instruction of that man."

Unfortunately, Rheticus had to return to his university teaching job and wasn't able to stay and oversee the printing. Rheticus asked Andreas Osiander, a Lutheran minister in Nuremberg, to take charge of the project. Osiander had experience overseeing the printing of books with lots of mathematical calculations. But Osiander had strong opinions about what he considered right and wrong. He believed that some of the things he read in Copernicus's book contradicted passages in the Bible that described the earth as standing still and the sun as moving. Without telling Rheticus—or Copernicus!—Osiander wrote an unsigned "letter to the reader" that he substituted for Copernicus's preface to the book. In it, he stated that *On the Revolutions* was just a hypothesis, and that it wasn't intended as the truth!

When Rheticus saw the printed book with Osiander's inserted comments, he was furious. He scratched out the lines in his copy of the book, but there was nothing further that could be done. The book was released the way it had been printed.

Osiander's insert may have affected how *On the Revolutions* was received throughout Europe. Many Protestants and Catholic scholars alike simply dismissed it. They thought if it was "just a hypothesis," then it wasn't worth making a fuss over. Many astronomers also rejected Copernicus's theory, at least initially. They admired all work he had done, and his careful calculations, but they continued to believe that the geocentric view of the universe was correct. Other astronomers, however, realized the importance of Copernicus's work and were inspired to build on his ideas; Galileo was one of them.

Copernicus may never have realized what Osiander had done. He was very ill, lying on his deathbed, when a copy of the book finally arrived at his house in 1543 CE. He may have been too sick even to hold it; we don't know. We also don't know how he would have responded to the criticisms *On the Revolutions* received. But something Copernicus wrote in the preface of the book that was put back in later editions, indicates that no matter what people thought, he knew he was right:

"Perhaps there will be babblers who, although completely ignorant of mathematics, nevertheless take it upon themselves to pass judgment on mathematical questions and, badly distorting some passages of Scripture to their purpose, will dare find fault with my undertaking and censure it. I disregard them even to the extent as despising their criticism as unfounded."

Portrait of Copernicus

Life and Achievements of Galileo

If Galileo were alive today as a child about your age, he would likely be a student who was constantly raising his hand in class to ask questions, offer opinions, and point out places where he thought the textbooks were wrong. Galileo grew up in a time when the ideas and writings of Aristotle and other ancient Greek and Roman scholars were **revered**. But Galileo did not hesitate to question authority. As a university student, his questioning nature even earned him the nickname "The Wrangler" because he asked so many questions and challenged many of Aristotle's theories about the way things worked in the natural world. It didn't help that he also had a reputation for being rather rude and arrogant! Yet although Galileo could be annoying, he was also very observant and had a gift for solving problems by conducting simple, but clever, experiments.

A Mathematical Mind

Galileo was born in Pisa, the Italian city now famous for its leaning tower. While studying medicine at the University of Pisa, he became fascinated by mathematics. Learning about it became an obsession, to the point where he abandoned his medical studies. He eventually became a mathematics professor at the University of Pisa. The job didn't pay well, but it suited Galileo's inquisitive mind and gave him the freedom to continue challenging ancient beliefs with experiments.

For example, in Galileo's time people believed that if you dropped two objects of different weights, the heavier object would fall faster and hit the ground first. They believed it because Aristotle had said so in his writings about how gravity worked. According to Aristotle, an object that weighs 10 pounds should fall 10 times faster than an object that weighs one pound.

But the more Galileo thought about this, the more he thought Aristotle was wrong. According to an account written by one of Galileo's students (which may or may not be true), Galileo decided to test Aristotle's theory on the Tower of Pisa. He climbed to the top with two metal balls—one small and one large. If Aristotle was correct about falling objects, Galileo said, the larger, heavier ball should strike the ground first. But Galileo believed that all objects, regardless of their weight, fall at the same rate. So, from the top of the tower, the story goes, Galileo released the balls while students and professors watched from below. Down the balls fell—and struck the earth with a thump at the exact same instant.

Galileo on the Tower of Pisa

A Weighty Test

If you try Galileo's experiment at home, use objects of similar shape, such as an orange and a grape. If you drop an orange and a piece of paper, the experiment won't work: the orange will fall quickly, but the piece of paper will float down slowly. That's because in this case something more than gravity is at work. The paper falls slowly because of air resistance. The flat surface of the paper presents a large area for the air to push against. If there were no air resistance—for example, if you conducted your experiment on the moon—then the orange and the sheet of paper would fall at the same rate.

In August 1971, David R. Scott, an astronaut on the Apollo 15 mission, tried such an experiment on the moon. He dropped a hammer and a feather, and they hit the moon's surface at the same time. "How about that," said Scott. "Mr. Galileo was correct!"

Even if Galileo didn't drop metal balls from the tower, his notebooks show that he conducted other experiments in which he dropped objects or rolled them down slanted surfaces. He then used mathematics to analyze the results of the experiments and draw conclusions about how gravity worked based on evidence. The significance of Galileo's gravity experiments went beyond learning more about this force, however. He'd proved that Aristotle was wrong, that a long-held belief simply wasn't true.

Galileo's pendulum clock, 1642 CE

Galileo went on to perform many other scientific experiments. He turned some of his discoveries into clever inventions. For example, he studied the steady motion of **pendulums** and ended up designing the first pendulum clock. He created a simple thermometer that could register changes in temperature. He invented a compass used for aiming canons so they could more accurately fire cannonballs.

Galileo's thermometer

It was with the telescope, though, that Galileo made his most important discoveries. He is sometimes mistakenly credited with inventing the telescope. He didn't—but he improved on the original design and built telescopes with increasingly high magnifying power. Thanks to his telescopes, and discoveries made by the Polish astronomer Nicolaus Copernicus, Galileo toppled the idea that the earth was at the heart of the solar system.

Copernicus, Kepler, and the View of the Heavens

As you read in Chapter 5, Copernicus took the first revolutionary steps toward overturning the geocentric model of the universe. Through careful observations of the night sky and mathematical calculations, Copernicus worked out that the earth, along with the other planets, orbits the sun. No one knows exactly when Galileo read Copernicus's book, *On the Revolutions of Heavenly Orbs*, which was printed in 1543 CE. In 1597 CE, however, Galileo corresponded with Johannes Kepler, a German astronomer who was also convinced, based on his observations, that the earth traveled around the sun. In one letter, Galileo acknowledged that he agreed with Copernicus. He also mentioned that publicly agreeing with Copernicus's ideas was a risky thing to do, because it went against accepted beliefs about the universe:

"....Like you, I accepted the Copernican position several years ago and discovered from thence the causes of many natural effects which are doubtless inexplicable by the current theories. I have written up many of my reasons and refutations on the subject, but I have not dared until now to bring them into the open, being warned by the fortunes of Copernicus..."

Yet once Galileo got his hands on a telescope, he couldn't keep quiet about what he was seeing in the night sky. Have you ever looked through a telescope at the stars? With the naked eye, the stars appear to be little more than bright points of light. But with a telescope, you can see the moons of Jupiter (just like Galileo!), the rings of Saturn, and individual stars in the Milky Way.

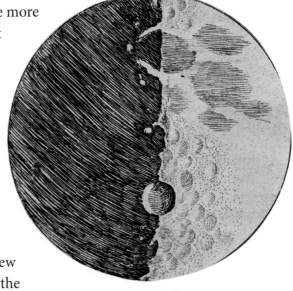

Galileo's drawing of the moon from *The Starry Messenger*

After publishing *The Starry Messenger* in 1610 CE, Galileo kept on making discoveries and kept on writing about them. He knew he risked angering officials in the Catholic Church because what he was finding contradicted beliefs that had been taught for more than a thousand years. But he did it anyway. He once said, "I do not feel obliged to believe that the same God who has **endowed** us with sense, reason, and intellect has intended us to forgo their use."

After his first brush with the Inquisition in 1616 CE, Galileo was more aware of how risky contradicting the Catholic Church could be. Yet he kept thinking, writing, and talking about the heliocentric model. For a time, influential friends and politicians who felt his discoveries were important were able to protect him. But when Galileo's book *Dialogue Concerning the Two Chief World Systems* came out in 1632 CE, it created an uproar.

In this book, Galileo did exactly what Pope Urban VIII had ordered him not to do. He compared Aristotle's and Ptolemy's ideas about the geocentric model to Copernicus's heliocentric model. The arguments he presented in the book led to one obvious conclusion: Copernicus was right. Furthermore, Galileo wrote the book in Italian rather than in Latin. All Italians who could read, not just highly educated scholars and specialists, were able to understand it. Galileo also presented the information in a clear and humorous way, so people wanted to read it. And they did! With the aid of the printing press, the book quickly got into the hands of many people.

This success backfired for Galileo. If the book had been written in Latin and stayed behind the walls of universities and monasteries, it would not have presented much of a threat. But because so many people were reading and talking about the book, Galileo's enemies became even more convinced that he had to be stopped. Church leaders worried that if ordinary people were allowed to question the Church's ideas about the universe, they might begin to question other teachings. The Protestant Reformation had already split the Church and set Protestant groups and Catholics against each other. With all the trouble Galileo was causing, the Church feared losing even more power and influence over its followers.

Galileo on Trial

In 1632 CE, when the Inquisition ordered Galileo to Rome to stand trial for heresy, he was a sick man of 70 years. He pleaded that he was too ill to make the trip. The pope was unmoved and insisted he come. Galileo had to be carried the entire way from Florence to Rome (about 170 miles) on a stretcher.

During his trial, Galileo was falsely accused of using trickery to get permission to write *Dialogue*. The inquisitors insisted that Galileo confess and take back his support for the ideas of Copernicus. Galileo knew that if he did not recant, he faced possible death. So, in 1633 CE, he publicly stated that the sun is not at the center of the universe and that the earth does not move.

Frontispiece of edition of Galileo's *Dialogue*, 1635 CE

The Inquisition punished Galileo by forcing him to live under guard in a house for the rest of his life. He could no longer publish or discuss his ideas, and his books were banned. As often happens with banned books, however, the already-popular *Dialogue* became a best seller almost overnight. It was distributed all over Europe and beyond.

Galileo did not spend the last years of his life dozing by a crackling fire. He was allowed visitors. He continued writing and completed an important book on physics. It summarized much of the scientific work he had done for the previous three decades of his life. A friend smuggled the manuscript to the Netherlands, where it was published. The Inquisition had forbidden Galileo to ever publish again, so he wrote an introduction to the book in which he claimed it had been printed without his knowledge. He referred to the book fondly as "the child of my brain."

Galileo is often called the father of modern astronomy, even of modern science. His discoveries and his writings certainly changed the world of science forever. He demanded that we learn about the universe around us by experimentation and observation. He insisted that theories be supported by evidence. He had the courage to question accepted authorities and pursue the truth.

Glossary

A

advocate, *v.* to act in favor of or on behalf of someone or something (**advocated**)

B

bequeath, *v.* to pass on property to someone in a will (**bequeathed**)

bind, *v.* to fasten two or more things together

C

calling, *n.* a strong urge to pursue a specific profession or way of life

cardinal, *n.* a leader in the Catholic Church who is chosen by the pope (**cardinals**)

censor, *v.* to examine and control the content of materials (**censored**)

clergy, *n.* people who are religious leaders and who perform religious ceremonies

condemn, *v.* to say in a strong or definite way that something is wrong or bad

confess, *v.* to admit you did something wrong (**confessed**)

congregation, *n.* the members of a church gathered for a religious ceremony

contemporary, *n.* a person living in the same time period and/or of the same age as another person (**contemporaries**)

contradict, *v.* to disagree with and go against a statement or action (**contradicted**)

contraption, *n.* a machine or device that is strange and/or complex

convert, *n.* a person who has changed his or her beliefs or changed religions (**converts**)

D

decree, *n.* an official order that must be followed (**decrees**)

defy, *v.* to go against; to refuse to obey (**defying**)

descend, *v.* to come down (**descended**)

devout, *adj.* devoted, especially to a specific religion or point of view

doctrine, *n.* a belief or set of beliefs held by a group of people

E

embrace, *v.* to welcome wholeheartedly (**embraced**)

endow, *v.* to give a quality or ability to (**endowed**)

extravagance, *n.* something that is expensive or wasteful and not a necessity

F

foe, *n.* enemy

H

heresy, *n.* beliefs or opinions that challenge, or go against, the beliefs or opinions of those in power

I

immoral, *adj.* going against the principles of right and wrong that are generally accepted by most members of a group

institution, *n.* an organization set up for a specific purpose

intervene, *v.* to come between; to prevent from happening (**intervened**)

L

lever, *n.* a strong, solid bar used to move or lift something

M

mechanism, *n.* **1.** a piece of machinery; **2.** parts that work together in a machine

O

order, *n.* a religious group with specific beliefs and practices (**orders**)

P

parchment, *n.* material made from animal skin and used as a writing surface

pendulum, *n.* a weight that swings regularly back and forth, often used to measure time in a clock (**pendulums**)

persecute, *v.* to treat someone unfairly or cruelly because of his or her religious beliefs (**persecuted**)

persecution, *n.* the act of treating someone unfairly or cruelly because of his or her religious beliefs

ponder, *v.* to think about deeply (**pondered**)

proof, *n.* **1.** evidence that something is true or correct; **2.** a test showing that a mathematic calculation is correct (**proofs**)

R

radical, *adj.* very disruptive to a widely accepted belief or idea

recant, *v.* to publicly take back an opinion expressed in the past

reform, *n.* an improvement (**reformers; reformation**)

revered, *adj.* looked up to; held in high esteem

revitalize, *v.* to give life to or energize again (**revitalizing**)

revolutionize, *v.* to completely change something (**revolutionized**)

rhythm, *n.* a regularly repeated motion or sound

S

salvation, *n.* the act of being saved from sin or danger

sect, *n.* a smaller group of people united by common religious beliefs that often contradict the beliefs of a larger group

secular, *adj.* not connected to religion

self-disciplined, *adj.* the ability to make yourself do what is necessary on your own without being told by someone else

shame, *n.* a negative feeling of embarrassment or regret

sin, *n.* an action that is considered morally wrong or that goes against religious teachings

speculation, *n.* an educated guess about something; not proven beyond doubt

spiritual, *adj.* of or related to religious beliefs and feelings

superior, *n.* a person in a higher position (**superiors**)

T

theology, *n.* the study of religion

theory, *n.* an explanation for why something happens based on evidence (**theories**)

thesis, *n.* a statement or idea (**theses**)

Core Knowledge®

Core Knowledge Language Arts®

Series Editor-In-Chief
E.D. Hirsch, Jr.

President
Linda Bevilacqua

Editorial Staff
Khara Turnbull, Editorial Director
Sarah Zelinke, Lesson Development Director
Rosie McCormick, Content Director
Deborah Samley, Managing Editor

Sara Hunt, Senior Editor
Erin Kist, Senior Editor

Angelica Blanchette, Associate Editor
Laura Drummond, Associate Editor
Liz Pettit, Associate Editor
Kate Stephenson, Associate Editor
Cate Whittington, Associate Editor

Editorial-Design Coordination
Robin Blackshire, Director, Editorial-Design Coordination

Mick Anderson, Senior Copy Editor
Nathan Baker, Copy Editor

Maggie Buchanan, Copy Editor
Emma Earnst, Web Content Manager
Lucinda Ewing, Copy Editor
James Kendley, Revisions and Documentation Specialist

Design and Graphics Staff
Scott Ritchie, Creative Director

Liza Greene, Art Coordinator
Liz Loewenstein, Print Production Artist
Bridget Moriarty, Content Designer
Lauren Pack, Content Designer
Amy Siever, Print Production Artist

Consulting Project Management Services
ScribeConcepts.com

Reader Authors

Rebecca L. Johnson

Deborah Mazzotta Prum

Expert Reviewer

Gerald P. Fogarty

Illustration and Photo Credits